PLAN
2 B U

"Wisdom is better than strength "
                    Solomon - Ecclesiastes

ISBN – 978-0-9917595-6-9

Malachi

PUBLICATIONS

http://malachibooks.weebly.com

TABLE of CONTENT

Introduction

Plan to be you! Often times, we want to go places, we want to accomplish things, we want to say things… but we either don't know how to go about it or we jut don't know where and how to start.

Some want an undergrad degree, some want a masters degree, other a doctorate degree.

Some are trying to get a house, acreage, a range or even just that simple cozy downtown condo.

For others, it's on the emotional side; want a good relationship with the right woman or the right man. Some want to fill that emptiness they feel.

For others, it's a total confusion, don't know where they are, but just want to get out and have a better lifestyle, become a better person with the right connections, the right people, you just want that good life.

Simple! You got to plan to be you!

In everything we do, we need a plan, an efficient yet easy plan to follow.

PLAN 2 B U, is about YOU. As you go about these pages, there will be a lot of "You" statements and "I" statements.

Why? Because it is about you. No sugar coating, no beating around the bush.

Plain and raw talk.

Straight to the point to be on point.

God Bless you.

"Suppose one of you wants to build a tower. Won't you first sit down and estimate the cost to see if you have enough money to complete it?"

Luke

Who am I?

This is a crucial question one needs to ask! Don't feel embarrassed or awkward.

Ask it – Who am I?

That is right, who are you? Do you know your self fully? Do you know yourself to some extent? Or you just don't know who you are at all.

"*I don't know*" is a correct answer. "*I don't know anymore*" is a correct answer too. The truth of the matter is, there is no right or wrong answer to these questions. However, it is important to know who you are if you want to go somewhere and if you want to establish a plan to become who you want to be and to go where you want to go!

Take out the scanner and scan yourself, your life and see whom you are.

The corky person will answer by giving their name. Fair enough. However, how silly can someone be? How ignorant can you really be?

Knowing who you are and answering this question is indeed the first step that will allow you get onto the right path.

Here, I will tell you who I was for starters! When I asked myself the question "Who am I?" over ten years ago, the answer I had was – I am a failure. Yes. That was my answer. I am a failure, I try and try and it doesn't work. I am done. I will leave life as it is and as it comes. I am done trying. I am done figuring out things.

I am a sinner. I am failure in my own definition.

I am sick and weak. I want to heal. My bones are shaking. I am trembling all over. How long will it take for me to heal?

I need help to be strong again. I need someone to make me strong.

I am so weak. I cried all night. My pillow is soaked; my bed is dripping wet from my tears. My enemies have caused me such sorrow that my eyes are worn out of crying.

I feel like a worm, less than human! People insult me and look down on me. Everyone who sees me makes fun of me. They shake their heads and stick out their tongues at me.

Trouble is near, and there is no one to help me. My enemies surround me like angry bulls. My strength is gone, like water poured out on the ground. My bones have separated. My courage is gone. My mouth is as dry as a piece of baked pottery.

I have many troubles. I have cried until my eyes hurt. My throat and stomach are aching. Because of my sin, my life is ending in grief; my years are passing away in sights of pain. My life is ending in weakness. My strength is draining away. My enemies despise me, and even my neighbors have turned away. When my friends see me in the street, they turn the other way. They are afraid to be around me. People want to forget me like someone already dead, thrown away like a broken dish. I hear them whispering about me. They have turned against me and plan to kill me.

PERSONAL NOTES

PERSONAL NOTES

PERSONAL NOTES

PERSONAL NOTES

PERSONAL NOTES

Who do I want to be?

Leadership – The action of leading a group or an organization. This is how Google defines it.

I am however convinced, that leadership means – leading yourself. I am a firm believer that everyone is a leader. If you are able to lead yourself accordingly, respectfully with integrity and will power, then you will be able to lead others.

I want to be a better person is a common phrase we hear and say. I want to be able to eat healthy; I want to be able to have a good relationship – none abusive. I want a better job, a better career.

We can seat here and write a list as tall as the Eiffel Tower. This is why I started with leadership. You have to lead yourself towards the goal you want to attain!

Easier said than done, is what comes to your mind. Fair enough. However, trust me, it is Easier done than said.

You must have heard the same line over, and over again – write it down, write who you want to be, have a vision board in your room or office. To be honest, I wouldn't recommend it. As we go farther, I will tell you what you need to write to get where you want to go!

Is there such a thing as a better person? I want to be a better person!

Yes!
I don't think you can be a better person, I know you can be a better person. I know you are a better person.

Look at it like a tree and its branches. The trunk of the tree is the main thing. The core. The branch is like a character trait.

A trait is an ingrained characteristic or habit that is difficult to learn or unlearn, like shyness or confidence.

Good traits that make you a better person are your generosity, integrity, devotion, self-control, faithfulness, determination, cooperation and spirituality.

Don't be proud of yourself and look down on everyone else.

Take a close read here:

Greedy people know only two things: "Give me," and "Give me." There are three other things that are never satisfied – the place of death, dry ground that needs rain, and a fire that will never stop by itself.

There are four things that are hard for me to understand – An eagle flying in the sky, a snake moving on a rock, a ship moving across the ocean, and a man in love with a woman.

On the other hand, there are four things that make trouble on the earth, the earth can not bear these, a slave who becomes a king, fools who have everything they need, a woman whose husband hated her but still married her, and a servant girl who becomes ruler over the woman she serves.

Here, it gets interesting, there are four things on earth that are small but very wise: Ants are small and weak, but they save their food all summer. Badgers are small animals, but they make their homes in the rocks. Locusts have no king, but they are able to work together. Lizards are small enough to catch with your hands, but you can find them lignin in kings' palaces.

Importance is something inevitable, there are two things that act important when they walk, a lion, he is the warrior of the animals and runs from nothing. A rooster walking around proudly.

Stirring milk causes butter to form. Hitting someone's nose causes blood to flow. And making people angry causes trouble.

Take time to search yourself…and answer the question – Who do I want to be?

PERSONAL NOTES

PERSONAL NOTES

PERSONAL NOTES

PERSONAL NOTES

PERSONAL NOTES

What can I do?

I wish it were that simple too. I ask for $ 1000.00 and it's given to me, no need to work. I knock at the Sheraton; the butler opens up a penthouse suite for me to rest. You get my point. It doesn't work like that.

In each and everything, you got to put in an effort to get a result. You got to put in energy. You put in negative energy ... well too bad; the end result is chaos. You put positive energy; chances are the end result will be beyond your expectations.

Every time you find work to do, do it the best you can. In the grave there is no work. There is no thinking, no knowledge, and there is no wisdom. And we are all going to the place of death.

Don't quit your job simply because the boss is angry with you. If you remain calm and helpful, you can correct even great mistakes.

If you dig a hole, you might fall into it. If you are moving large stones, they might hurt you. If you cut down a tree, you are in danger of it falling on you. But wisdom will make any job easier. It is very hard to cut with a dull knife. But if you sharpen the knife, the job is easier. Someone might know how to control snakes. But that skill is useless if a snake bites when that person is not around.

Do good wherever you go. After a while, the good you do will come back to you. Invest what you have in several different things. You don't know what bad things might happen on earth. There are some things you can be sure of. If clouds are full of rain, they will pour water on the earth. If a tree falls—to the south or to the north—then it will stay where it falls.

But there are some things that you cannot be sure of. You must take a chance. If you wait for the perfect weather, you will never plant your seeds. If you are afraid that every cloud will bring rain, you will never harvest your crops.

You don't know where the wind blows. And you don't know how a baby grows in its mother's womb. In the same way, you don't know what God will do—and he makes everything happen.

So begin planting early in the morning, and don't stop working until evening. You don't know what might make you rich. Maybe everything you do will be successful.

It is good to be alive. It is nice to see the light from the sun. You should enjoy every day of your life, no matter how long you live. But remember that you will die, and you will be dead much longer than you were alive. And after you are dead, you cannot do anything.

PRAY your way into your destiny. Have FAITH, believe and PRAY. There is no other alternative. Don't get caught up with the theories that you hear everywhere…the wellbeing strategies.

PERSONAL NOTES

PERSONAL NOTES

PERSONAL NOTES

PERSONAL NOTES

PERSONAL NOTES

How do I do it?

This is the big question. How do I do it?
How do I plan my life to become ME. How do I
go about planning so I can be that better person?

The answer is very simple, in three words: PRAY
FOR IT. Talk to the Rock of Ages. There is no
other way to word it. I cannot stress the
importance of prayer life.

Some of you might say, "why do I have or why do
I need to pray. I don't believe in God, I do my
own thing. I hear that prayer is important for
certain things I can do it on my own. I go to
church when I have to."

I respect your reasoning and understanding.
However, as I mentioned earlier, I am not here to
sugar coat the realities of life. You don't have a
prayer life, you will crash sooner or later. Only
prayer can feel the emptiness you experience in
life.

A high paying job will buy houses; cars; clothes; bags; jewelry; vacations… name it. But money will never fill the emptiness you feel in your life. Money won't buy you a marriage. It may get you a wedding but not a marriage!

Prayer on the other hand, will draw the many things that you are missing or want to improve at many levels. Intellectual, emotional, material, physical, health … again… name anything you can think of, prayer will take care of it.

I know that some of you will say: So if I pray, is prayer going to go buy me bread?

Please, don't laugh, it may sound funny, sound stupid, but it is not. Yes, prayer will provide the channel for you to get bread, milk, eggs, butter, sugar, tea and coffee. That is right, prayer will generate a life of challenges but also a life of abundance and peace. The good thing is that for the challenges, you will always find the answer in prayer!

Take a look at some best selling authors and books like Think and Grow Rich by Napoleon

Hill, Rich Dad Poor Dad by Robert Kiosaki, The Personal MBA-Master the art of business by Josh Kufman.

Take for example Henri Fayol (1841-1925) who from his perspective considers management to consist of six functions: Forecasting, planning, organizing, commanding, coordinating, and controlling. He was one of the most influential contributors to modern concepts of management.

In the bible, Forecasting is well explained, well illustrated in the book of proverbs.

Planning is well illustrated in the entire bible, as you will see throughout this booklet.

Organizing is also mentioned several times in the bible! In Corinthians: But all things should be done decently and in order.

You get the point, READ YOUR BIBLE!

In regards to command, it is obvious. Read Exodus, Leviticus, Deuteronomy, Numbers,

Nehemiah, Joshua, 1 Kings, 2 Samuel and many more.

Pay close attention to the principals explained in those books. Then go in the bible and search, you will find those principles.

My point, The word of God – Jesus-Christ, is beyond human intellect. Hence the reason why all these major guys use the biblical principles, tweak them to their advantage and seem so wise by writing it in terms that a business oriented person would prefer reading.

Don't fall into the trap. Put God – Jesus-Christ first in your life. Then PRAY, and then let everything unfold.

It is amazing how we give so much credit to NASA, Neil Armstrong, Buzz Aldin, Michael Collins and the Mars pathfinder's sojourner Rover for the discoveries and exploits done but we don't seem to give the credit if not the honor and acclamation to the one who created the heavens and the earth. We get so caught up, that some of us have no idea that Adam was the first human on earth. We instead come up with all sorts of theories, analogies and the other "gies" one might come up with.

Have you ever wondered why at every burial, the priest, the pastor, the clergy, always says – You came from dust, and to dust you return.

Certain things in our world or life are inevitable. We are so accustomed by so many events and forget that everything started somewhere. We forget that there was a trigger for this cycle to occur in a specific manner. The discovery of Science, Biology, Chemistry, Mathematics; in order words the discovery of these principles have made humanity ignorant if not made us a proud civilization. We refuse to accept that God owns it all and created it all, and that is including you and me. The animals, the universe, the wonderful four seasons and even the beautiful and majestic rainbow!

Today, I am writing in English, but no one is capable of saying where our language originated from yet it is so crystal clear and specific that due to our silly self, we don't know anymore. God had to control us and set the record straight and created all these languages that are spoken on the earth.

Divine protection and guidance is something we still hardly believe is genuine. We still rely at maximum capacity that the gun, the riffle and the alarm system at home will protect us. I m not starting a firearm control debate but I know, I believe and I testify that the Lord protects; the Great I Am. Don't get caught up by the act or symbol but get caught up in the FAITH!

It does not matter where we may be. The stage we are in life. As long as we trust, believe and follow Him, it is eminent that He leads the way. No matter how lost, confused or clueless one may be. Whether it's in life, at work, at school… the Pillar of Cloud and the Pillar of Fire will permanently guide and direct us. The human memory can be very selective. However, this is where things are fascinating with Jesus-Christ. He will remind you of all His deeds and take you to destination so you are in the correct mind set.

Ability is defined as possession of the means or skill to do something. Ability may refer to super power; super human ability. The ability to do various things comes by PRAYER and FASTING! This is as good as unveiling the sequence to a fortified password. When you PRAY and FAST… something is meant to happen.

Like a lost sheep our generation and civilization is. Fortunate, Blessed we are that the Son of Man has come to save that which was lost. Looking back, looking ahead, it is amazing to see that where a group of individuals agree on something, believe in it and pursue it with the same intensity, they somehow always achieve.

Everyone talks about peace. World Peace. Good, but honestly, we are shooting amiss. That is, we gather mostly in the name of peace, gather in the name of love, gather in our own names and gather for so many other motives yet the key to unlock it all, the key to melt the ice of all these tensions is simple. We just need to bind it here on earth; we need to gather in the name of the Most High God, in the name of Jesus-Christ.

In this age of ours, some may see the Ten Commandments as irrelevant because we leave in and are part of a modern society.

Yet the commandments that God gave are still very vital to this age! You need to remember this – the word of God shall never return void, His word does not expire, its always fulfilling. If it did, then why are we holding on to the promises the Lord gave the children of Israel?
When it comes to the commandments, we try to alter things. It is written that my people die for lack of knowledge!

Look at our society; look at it crumbling apart like the Oklahoma City bombing of April 1995. It is said, it is instructed it is commanded that we should have no other god before Him (Jesus-Christ) yet today we indulge in various religions, various meditation things and search for gods we don't know, gods that are not gods, gods that we create ourselves.

You shall not take the name of the Lord your God in vain, yet today swears with the name of Jesus are the most popular.

Honor your father and your mother, that your days may be long upon the land which the Lord your God is giving you. Today, men and women find it normal to curse at their parents, engage in physical and verbal abuse towards their parents. Isn't it God that gave us the breath of life? Isn't it Him who can take it back too?

You shall not murder … our jails are crowded with murderers; we wage war against nations to kill. We plot to kill.

You shall not commit adultery; today our society takes pleasure in sexuality like it's a religion. Married men and women going around, bed hoping, and then wonder why things are tough, wonder why so many weird diseases.

The Ten Commandments I believe is a foundation, a principle, a rule to abide with and excel in. We still tend to think that God is human; we often if not always limit God!

With men, most things can be impossible, but with God all things are possible.

Often times when things, when life has lost direction we hope for and remember the better days. When the "better" days arrive, do we take time to be thankful, or are we caught up with the good life of that moment?

The admiration I have for King David is his dedication, truthfulness and commitment to the Lord. To read and hear him extol the Lord is a solace. We say we are deep in love, when that deepness is present indeed, never will the love fade.

When troubles arise, when troubles come our way, we tend to lose ourselves. This is Christian or non-Christian alike. We forget our substance! We are quick to respond with enthusiasm that the just live by faith when things are going our way.

Yet, when the trial comes, many calm down and forget who they are, many are ashamed of the gospel when they are put in awkward situations by non-Christians, but is it not written that For I am not ashamed of the gospel of Christ, for it is the power of God to salvation for everyone who believes. This is the time indeed, this is the moment, and despite all the trials and tribulation we face in society to say: The just live by FAITH.

I have FAITH. I have FAITH in Jesus-Christ. I believe in Jesus-Christ. I have FAITH things will work out. I have FAITH that one day these trials and tribulations shall end. It is obvious that FAITH triumphs in times of trouble. Tribulation produces perseverance; and perseverance produces character; and character produces hope.

Now hope does not disappoint, because the Holy Spirit who was given to us has poured out the love of God in our hearts. With all this being said and proven, where is your FAITH? In God? In your money? In your education? At your place of employment?

Without FAITH it is impossible to please God, for he who comes to God must believe that He is, and that he rewards those who diligently seek Him.

PRAYER and FAITH! The key, the passcode to life.

Now this is the confidence that we have in Him-Jesus-Christ our Lord and Savior. That if we ask for anything according to His will, He hears us. And if we know that He hears us, whatever we ask, we know that we have the petitions that we have asked of Him.

Remembering all these wonderful things is good but it also time to act. It is time to press on. Evening and morning and at noon I will pray, and cry aloud and He shall hear my voice.

PERSONAL NOTES

PERSONAL NOTES

PERSONAL NOTES

PERSONAL NOTES

PERSONAL NOTES

Conclusion

Plan to be you. PRAY FOR IT. Prayer is the answer to everything and anything. For some, prayer is hard; prayer is complex. However, in order to be able to successfully Plan 2 B U, you need to pray. Prayer and faith will lead you in the right path.

How do I get to Pray the right way? Well, you can follow the template of the Lords prayer for one, read the Holy Bible to get inspiration, to know the word of God, to understand the principals of life.

The more you read your bible; you will see prayers shaping up. In the bible you will find the secrets of finances, hence giving you the correct elements for your financial stability. In the bible you will find the secrets to a healthy relationship, how to deal with anxiety, stress and many other things. This will also shape the way you pray in regards to different things you are experiencing in life.

Not having a sincere prayer life, a sincere life of prayer will be evident. You will be accustomed to adultery, fornication, sin, profanity, idolatry, sorcery, hatred, contentions, jealousies, outbursts of wrath, selfish ambitions, dissensions, heresies, envy, murders, drunkenness, revelries, and the like.

It's simple, if you sow the bad, you will reap it too, corruption and more.

On the other hand, prayer, will bring forth love, joy, peace, kindness, goodness, faithfulness, gentleness, self-control...and many more. Sow the good, take the opportunity to do good things.

As it is written by Paul in Ephesians, "I pray that the Lord God of our Lord Jesus Christ, the Father of glory, may give to you the spirit of wisdom and revelation in the knowledge of Him, the eyes of your understanding being enlightened; that you may know what is the hope of His calling, what are the riches of the glory of His inheritance in the saints, and what is the exceeding greatness of His power toward us who believe, according to the working of His mighty power which He worked in Christ when He raised Him from the dead and seated Him at His right hand in the heavenly places, far above all principality and power might and dominion, and every name that is named, not only in this age but also in that which is to come. And He put all things under His feet, and gave Him to be head over all things to the church, which is His body, the fullness of Him who fills all in all.

The grace of our Lord Jesus Christ be with your spirit. Amen.

You, me, us, should not be ashamed of the gospel of Christ, for it is the power of God the salvation for everyone who believes. For the righteousness of God is revealed form faith to faith as it is written:

The Just shall live by faith.

My Lord; My God; My savior.
You the Lord who knows the way of the
righteous.
My shepherd; my light and my salvation.
My refuge and My fortress.

In you I trust

PRAY and PRAY again

Oh Lord, you my defender, you my strength. You are my salvation.

I proclaim your name, you does thing beyond what glorious means, and I exalt your name.

You are my refuge. In financial distress, you kept me. You are a safe place, a shelter, a home that gives me comfort, affection, love and hope.

When the wind blows my way, I stand and raise my hands to you Lord. I call you Lord and you answer me. When the storm catches me by surprise in hopes of toppling me…again Lord, you shield me, you direct and lead me out of the storm. The storm remains alone and confuses itself as I am long gone into a place of safety, your mighty hands.

I trust in you Lord. I am confidant and reassured that I am safe in you. You are not like the human stock market that is unpredictable! You are the Rock of Ages, the Chief Cornerstone! The great I AM.

O Lord of Hosts, you the God of Israel, I pray to you because you are the only one true God. You have made the heaven and the earth. You have created me.

Hear me out Lord, I know I have a life with a purpose, with a mission. I know I have been appointed by you to do wonders in your name.

When tough situations arise in my life, I am not shaken, I am not scared because You are the one who makes a way through the sea And a path through the mighty waters.

When my person is attacked, my reputation is attacked, I threat not because you are my vindicator.

Guide me in Your truth and teach me the way. Give me wisdom, knowledge and understanding. Give me the success that you hold in store for the upright. Be my shield Lord.

Give me wisdom so I do not end up in the ways of wicked men who delight in doing wrong. Give me strength to bind love and faithfulness around my neck so it never leaves me.

I do not want to lean on my own understanding. I trust in you Lord with all my heart and I submit all my ways, my projects, my thoughts to you so you may make my paths straight.

Do not hide Your commandments form me Lord. May your lovingkindness come to me Lord. Your salvation according to Your promise. Teach me good discernment and knowledge, for I believe, trust and rely on your commandments.

I am yours Lord, save me. Like Jacob who named Bethel. I declare my being Bethel. Dwell in me Lord. I know you will never forsake me. I am seeking you Lord. And I know I have found you.

I love you Lord, but I know you loved me first and I know I am blessed and thank you for granting me your grace.

READ and READ again the Bible. Everything is in it. The reverent fear of the Lord, that is, worshiping Him and regarding Him as truly awesome is the beginning and the preeminent part of knowledge, its starting point and its essence.

Have you considered the richest men and women, how did they become so rich? Also, have you checked the poor people, how did they become poor? The rich and the poor were given the opportunity to make decisions and the decisions they make yielded what they are today.

The decision you make now determine your tomorrow. Whether you want to be rich or not, have a good future or a bad one, it all depends on the decisions you are making now. God has given mankind a great power, which is the ability to make decisions.

We make decisions in every area of our lives; we make career decisions, business decisions, financial decisions, and spiritual decisions. We even make marital decisions, who we want to spend the rest of our lives with. The decisions we make now, great or small will affect our lives one way or the other. Research shows that an average adult makes over 5000 decisions in a day some of which are relevant and while others are not. There is a vast number of characters that made good decisions in the Bible. The sons of Levi made a decision to be on the Lord side in Exodus 32:26.

At one time of our lives, we have to make decisions. But before making a decision, what are the things you should consider?

To every action, there are consequences and to make an action, you must have made a decision. Achan made a very bad decision in Joshua 7, he took accursed things from war and he had to face the consequences, he was killed alongside his family. You have to think about what the end might bring before taking any decision.

Samson, a very popular man in the Bible also took a wrong decision. He took a wife from the land he was told not to marry from. The decision cost his life, he died with his enemies.

I will leave you with this; Some old men were once interviewed, they were asked what they would like to get back if they were given the opportunity to get something from their past.

Almost all of them, about 80% said they would love to get their time back. Time is the only thing you lost and never get back for the rest of your life. Even if you are the purest of all and you pray to God to get back the time you have wasted, the prayer can never be answered.

You can only be given an opportunity to use another time to get things right. If there's any area of life you should be wishing to improve and build yourself on, it should be the ability to manage time. Many of us want to become great in life, we want to be the boss of either our own business or a company we are employed to, we want to manage businesses, a company, or people but yet we can't manage time.

Even all these, managing business, job, people, or company requires a special training for effectiveness. Managing time is not like that, it doesn't require any special training. All it requires is discipline. You know your plans, and when you want to do them, so you don't need anyone to tell you when. "Time is the most valuable coin in your life. You and you alone will determine how that coin will be spent. Be careful that you do not let other people spend it for you."

For us to get to understand the importance of time, we must at least know the meaning of time. So what is time?

Time has been defined and explained by different people but the most fitting for time is, time is a plan, schedule, or arrange of when something should happen or be done. Time is also what separates when everything should happen or be done.

There is a time for everything, and a season for every activity under the heavens:"

Everything we do under the heavens, on this earth, there's time. A time to be born and a time to die, a time to plant and a time to harvest, a time to weep and a time to laugh, a time for peace and a time for war, a time to work and a time to relax.

Everything has a time specific time. There's a time you were a kid, you do the things of a child, you behave childishly, and now that you are growing or grown, you then put away the childish things that you do. That's because you know that there is time to start behaving maturely.

"When I was a child, I talked like a child, I thought like a child, I reasoned like a child. When I became a man, I put the ways of childhood behind me."

There is time to plant and there is time for harvest. You cannot skip the time to plant and jump into the time of harvest; it is not possible. There are young billionaires nowadays, they are very rich not only because they have the mentality or training on how to start a business and make it blossom.

The important thing we must learn from them is that they used their time properly. They invested in their time, they have spent the early of their lives managing their time, they know when to study, when to meditate, when to work, and when to relax. They had planted when it was time to plant, and they are in the time of harvest. There's something you must know, the time to plant is not much, it might just be few years, but the time of harvest might take a lifetime. You will continue to reap the fruit of your labor, the fruit of what you have spent time doing.

We sometimes think about how we can pray before going to work because we are always in a rush. If we kneel down to pray or worship, we might get late to work, so what then can we do because we have to keep time balance.

Sometimes, we rush in the morning because we wake up late and we want to get to work or anywhere early so we think we have missed the proper time to pray. Prayer is a communication between you and God, you can be in a rush and still pray while doing the chores or dressing up. It is just like you making a phone call while you are in a rush.

God understands you, all you just need is create time to talk to him. No matter how little the prayer is, God hears and he will do according to what you have said. What is important is your heart, it doesn't matter the duration of your prayer. There are people that pray for hours and yet their prayers are baseless, when you make your request known to God from your heart, he will surely answer because he looks the heart.

You can be there saying you don't have time to study, you don't even have time read the Bible or you don't have time to relax. The truth of the matter is that there's no time for anything, you create time for something. You create time out of no time.

"Nothing happens all the time, even time is timed." No time duration is short, set time for study, find time to relax during the day, set time to read the word of God even if it's just a verse daily. It helps a lot and doing this you place everything in its right time and there would be no time conflict.

Even after saying there's no time for anything, there are things that waste time still which you must deal with for you to manage your time and use it effectively.

When you lack discipline, you will never cherish time or know the importance of time management.

"No discipline seems pleasant at the time, but painful. Later on, however, it produces a harvest of righteousness and peace for those who have been trained by it."

It's a very hard time at the time of discipline, but you just have to do it for the sake the reward. Anybody that his or her work starts early in the day, will set an alarm and with time, he or she get used to the time. That's an example of disciplining oneself.

You can't start sleeping more than the expected time, you will the consequence. When you don't set time for yourself to pray, you pray at the wrong time and you don't pray at the right time. Lack of discipline leads to the next thing that wastes time.

As it is written in the Bible that *"there is a time to sow and a time to reap,"* if you are lazy and you don't utilize the available time to sow, you will not harvest anything. Don't be lazy laziness kills time and makes it a total waste.

When you are lazy, you start procrastinating. Procrastination is nothing but a sin.

"Remember, it is sin to know what you ought to do and then not do it."

When you procrastinate, you use the time that could have been used for another purpose. When you shift the time of planting forward, you also shift the time of harvest forward. Time waits for no man, once you don't get it done at right time, you get it done at the right time again.

Time management is the most important thing we must train ourselves to do. We must learn to set plans. Even when God was creating the heaven and earth, he had plans; he didn't take the time of one for the other. When it was time to create the light, he did, when it was time to create the living things, he did, and when it was time to rest, he did. He scheduled all, and he rested. Don't say you don't have time to relax. God could have just stopped at the sixth day, but he created the seventh day just to rest. Create time out of no time, and you will enjoy the reward later.

PLAN 2 B U

PERSONAL NOTES

PERSONAL NOTES

PERSONAL NOTES

PERSONAL NOTES

PERSONAL NOTES

PERSONAL NOTES

PERSONAL NOTES

PERSONAL NOTES

PERSONAL NOTES

PERSONAL NOTES

PERSONAL NOTES

Reference

Who am I?

Psalm 6 –

Psalm 22

Psalm 31

Who do I want to be?

Prov. 30

What can I do?

Ecclesiastes

How do I do it? –

Genesis 1 vs 1,10,

Genesis 8 vs 22,

Genesis 9 vs 16,

Genesis 11 vs 6,

Exodus 3 vs 14,

Exodus 12 vs 12,13,

Exodus 13 vs 21, 22,

Matthew 16 vs 9, 10, 11,

Matthew 17 vs 20,

Matthew 18 vs 11,

Matthew 18 vs 18-20,

Hosea 4:6,

Exodus 20,

Matthew 19 vs 26,

Romans 1 vs 16, 17,

Romans 5 vs 1-5,

Hebrews 11 vs 6,

1 John 3:23,

Psalm 55:17

Conclusion –

Galatians 5 vs 16 to 26, 6 vs 7 to 10, 6 vs 18;

Ephesians 1 vs 17 to 23,

Psalm 1, 5, 23, 91

Ecclesiastes 3:1

Corinthians 13:11

James 5:16

2 Samuel 16:7

Hebrews 12:11

James 4:17